A Subshade Variant
brought to you by
Cold Hat Productions

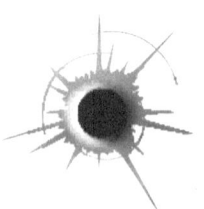

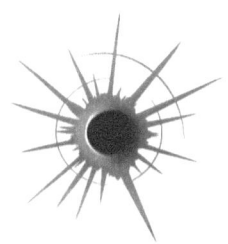
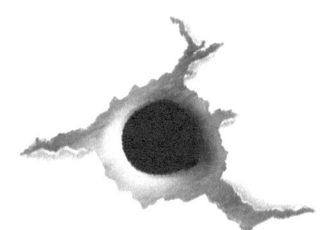

Henry Rifle's Greatest Hits

Silver Bullets and Random Misfires
The Capital Record Years
1998–2010

Produced by Flat Sole Studio
www.flatsolestudio.com

Copyright © 2023 Dan Hendrickson

All rights reserved. No part of this publication may be reproduced in whole or in part without written permission of the publisher.

Library of Congress Cataloging-in-Publication Data
Library of Congress Control Number: 2020944780
ISBN: 978-1-0880-8494-6 (paperback)
ISBN: 978-1-0880-8495-3 (ebook)

Photo Credits
Warren Strandell
Francine Corcoran
Marty Jonason

Original Artwork
Deb Sjurseth
Christina Smith

Book and Cover Design
Flat Sole Studio

To John Oakhurst and to A., W, S

"Everybody loves me. Most people just don't know it yet."
—Henry Rifle

A Note from the Author

The Capital Record Years were heady days. They were also the best of times and the worst of times. There were stretches where my life was like a giant Pina Colada and stretches where it felt like I was trapped inside a blender—stuck on frappe. In other words, they were a blur, a blur that left me a far more liquid being.

But what I'll remember most about those days, besides the endless battles with the label, is the work that came out of this turbulent period. This collection is composed of the very best of the very best. All the highlights, with the lowlights consigned to their rightful place on the cutting room floor.

I truly hope you enjoy it.

A Note for Readers

Henry Rifle was a pen name chosen long ago by me, Dan Hendrickson. It was a dummy corporation created by a fool. At the time of its (his) inception, I was mired in thick layers of overlaying sediment; a naturally shy person with—perhaps—a few things to say, somebody who couldn't find the courage to say/write those words myself.

Henry Rifle became the vehicle for all of those things I wanted to say and many of the things I thought I wanted to be. He wore sunglasses . . . he was edgy. He could say outlandish things about the world I was seeing and I was never blamed for them (not once!). On the contrary, as a friend once told me, "Henry Rifle is more popular than you are." Which was a strange thing to say, but rang true (now and then). Even so, like a hermit crab that outgrows its shell, I eventually had to scurry away from my own paper-thin creation. By then, a calcified shell had hardened around me and I was finally ready to embrace both sides of the person I was (and am): the detached hipster who prefers to observe from the shadows, and the farm boy* who cannot help but lead with his heart.

These are some of the stranger things I wrote, back in those days when I thought I was at least somewhat moderately cool.

*EDITOR'S NOTE: I've never lived on a farm. But I have milked a goat.**

**EDITOR'S NOTE: I've never milked a goat.

A Word from Management
A ghost is a ghost.
That's the deal.
If you don't like it,
form a union.
Or write somebody a letter.
Better yet, stuff a message
in a bottle
and toss it
in the ocean.
Depending upon
the winds and the tides,
we'll get right back to you.

How to Win Friends and Influence People
I haven't the first idea.
But some guy wrote a book about this
very thing, once.
Can't think of the fellow's name.
Andy . . . Andy—Andrew!
Yes!
Andrew Barnaby Jones.
I never forget a name.
Which is not at all to say
I haven't tried.

Gated Reverb
For a long time,
something was off.
Something
just wasn't right.
Like a donut without a hole,
my work, my sound,
it wasn't quite rock
and it wasn't quite roll.
Then I finally stitched
it all together: I got
a double-tracked soul.

How to be a Writer—Part 1

by Henry Rifle

Nobody has ever asked me how to be a writer, which . . . is a pretty big hint if you stop to think about it (which I never do). So I woke up one day and thought, *"You know what? I'm going to tell America how to be a writer anyway—simply because."* Now, I don't want to flood you with information. That's the last thing I want. No, I'm going to dole out my wisdom in dribs and drabs. The first thing you need to know if you want to be a writer? Gravitas rhymes with rabbit toss.

Here endeth the lesson (for now).

Holiday Christmas Wishes—2002
From the desk of
Henry J. Rifle

Dearest Chums,

First of all, I'm only sending out a handful of these sweet babies, because, frankly, I don't have the time. I have a very finite amount of patience and once that's gone, you can just cancel Christmas, Virginia! Besides, if I was going to send out an email to every fella I ever threw down a shot of rye with or every dame I ever smooched, I'd be here until doomsday. So if anyone comes around and starts whining and moaning and says, *"How come that no-good, S.O.B. Henry Rifle didn't send ME a Christmas card?"* tell 'em to piss off, direct from me, would you?

Now, then . . . as you may or may not have noticed, these are very uncertain times we're living in—VERY uncertain. One minute, you're on top of the world . . . the next, the world has you upside-down by the ankles and it's giving you the swirly of your life! These are hard times we're living through and, as I've said all along, it's a junkyard planet we're spinning on—not to mention a big ball of mud. Stick around long enough and you're bound to get dirty.
All that aside, this is the Yule season and we must try and be happy no matter how impossible that may be. What with the economy and rising gas prices, who knows what's going to happen next? And for God's sake, who's going to save the whales? This is exactly the kind of stuff I'm talking about. Frankly, I'm beginning to wonder if anyone has ever said anything. And if they did, who was listening?! Not me, that's for damn sure.

So once again I must implore you to enjoy this festive Holiday Season! What do you have to lose? We all know there's no Santa Claus. That doesn't mean he's a bad guy per se, but would you trust him with your kids? Exactly.

Henry Rifle

In closing, please rest assured that, if nothing else—if nothing else at all—I shall remain your friend from today forward, until the sun belches its last gasp of cosmic fury into this morning breath solar-system we call home.

All the best to you and yours,

Sincerely,
Henry J. Rifle

Shooting Gallery

"Some guys are pistols. I'm a buffalo gun."
—Henry Rifle

U.S. $3.50

Shooting Gallery

by Henry Rifle

Honest
I sometimes like to wear stupid hats.
Abraham Lincoln did, too,
and look where it got him:
Dead in a box.
I forget my point.

Bright and Early
It used to be I'd get up each morning,
light a cigarette and read the newspaper.
Lately, though, I've been
lighting the newspaper
and reading my cigarette.
It saves me a bunch of time,
and I'm feeling much better
about myself
and the world in general.

Broken Loom
Recently, I stopped having dreams.
I told my Native American friend
about it.
He told his grandfather.
His grandfather said it's because
my soul is dead.
Great.
That's all I need.

For the Record
Musically speaking, John Lennon was
probably my favorite genius.
I disagree with him, though, when he said
The Beatles were bigger than Jesus.
Granted, they sold more albums.
But I still say if anyone manages
to get Jesus into the recording studio . . .
he's gonna sell a pile
of records.

On Being a Bird
If the only thing I had to do
was fly around all day
and crap on people,
I'd sing, too.
I'd sing my damn lungs out!

Space Monkey
I read an article recently
that said the Russians
once sent a monkey into space.
If you ask me, that's sound policy.
I think we should keep doing that
every now and again,
just to show the monkeys
who's boss.

"My dreams are clean. Most of them have been filtered—through a drain."
—Henry Rifle

Seuss
The strange cat
walks into the sun.
His heart is a hat
and everyone laughs.

Holdout
He sits in his room
typing his commie poems.
Outside, the Capitalist Dogs bark furiously,
chained to a master they can't see.
"*Soon, America,*" he mutters, "*you will pay!
My poems will bring you to your knees!*"
He giggles insanely,
crushes out his cheap Russian cigarette
and lights another.
The night is young.

Norwegian Weird
This new guy moved into
my apartment building,
so I dropped by and had
a few words with him.
I decided he was a real nutball.
Later, I found he was Norwegian
and spoke very little English.
I decided to take a Norwegian course
and then chatted him up again
one fine afternoon.
I was right the first time.
The guy's a real nutball.

Jump
I was playing checkers with
my Chinese pal awhile back.
(Not Chinese Checkers).
Halfway through the game,
he built a wall of dominoes
across the middle of the board.
We sat there for a long time,
just staring down at the pieces.
Then we shrugged, got up,
went down to a club,
drank two pails of Sake,
and danced the night away
with these Swedish gals we met.

Japanese Applicant
When I got back from my job interview,
my friend asked me if I was the only
one they interviewed.
"*No*," I said, "*it was me and some Japanese guy.*"
She looked at me sadly and said,
"*What kind of job was it?*"

Je ne sais pas
I dreamt I was
in France last night,
but I didn't have my passport,
so they made me wake up.

Not quite exactly what I wanted
When I was seven,
all I got for Christmas
was a gift for understatement.
It was a bit of a letdown.

The Wheels of Fate
I used to have a friend who said
only sissies looked both ways
before crossing the street.
Of course, he's dead now.

What Goes Around
This kid I used to pick on in high school
went on to become a brilliant engineer.
Today, the Mississippi River
runs through my living room.

Down with MI 5
I once spent two months
in the Arizona desert
disguised as a cactus.
I can't tell you why.
Let's just say
the British Government owes me,
and leave it at that.

I'd much prefer a gift certificate
My uncle's a philosopher.
Every year for my birthday
he gives me something to think about.
The cheap son of a bitch.

One for the Kids
There's more to being cool than
driving fast and
smoking cigarettes.
Trust me.
I've crunched the numbers.

Simpatico
Sitting by the lake,
I hear the cry of the loon.
I know, baby.
I know.

Wading Pool
Bad poems are as common
as raindrops.
But you can sink into
a good poem.
And a great poem
can drown you.

Experiments in Blue
There are days my heart is as light
as a Japanese kite,
and nights you'd need a submarine
to explore the depths
of my sadness.
The difference, I think, is the sun.
Often the moon just makes
blues deeper.

Reflection
I like having
my picture taken
with the moon.
It makes me seem
more mysterious.

Companero

The moon has been a friend
over the years.
We've walked home together
many nights alone.

The Moon, Take Two

If someone offered me a ride
to the moon,
I'd be out the door.
I wouldn't even stop to make sandwiches.
I've been itching to get up there since 1969,
the year Neil Armstrong blew it.
Yeah, ol' Neil had the perfect chance
to rub Russia's collective face in it,
and he let it go in favor of that dumb line
of his.
Some nonsense about a giant step for mankind.
If I would have been the first person on the moon,
I'd have done a little moonwalk—you know,
backwards.
That would have shown them commies.
Then I would have gotten right up in the camera
and shouted, "In your face, baby! In your face!
That's right: it's us; the good, old U S of A,
coming to you live, from Moonland!
How you like us now?!"
Sigh.
My genius is totally wasted.

A Lunch Date
I met my friend for lunch today
for the second time in a month.
She's a girl and married.
Controversial stuff here.
Halfway through our meal, she said,
"*Now that we've been seen together twice
in public, I suppose people will think that
you're screwing me.*"
"*Yes,*" I replied gravely, "*and the fact
that I'm telling them the same
isn't going to help either.*"
She looked at me for about three seconds.
and then we both laughed like hell.
I like my friend.
But only as a friend.

A Cover Letter
Dear Madam or Sirs,
My name is Henry Rifle
and I am a poet, a scholar,
and a gentleman.
In other words, I am unemployed.
Can I have a job?
I haven't had a drink in days.
I sure could use one.
—a job, that is.
I promise I won't screw up too much.
You never know, there's a chance
I might not disappoint you.

Sincerely,
—*Henry*

Tips from The Master
The Zen Master pulled me aside
and told me I was in mortal danger.
*"There are ghosts in your eyes
and daggers in your heart,"* he said solemnly.
*"Unless these are dealt with—and soon
—you are not long for this world."*
"What shall I do about the daggers?" I asked.
He replied, *"Remove them one by one
and lay them down."*
"And about the ghosts in my eyes?"
"Visine," he said,
with a mischievous grin.

Most Things Are
"Where you been?" my roommate asked.
"Down by the river," I said, *"talking
to the Zen Master."*
"Zen master," he said dismissively.
"Yeah, right!"
"He is too a Zen Master," I replied calmly.
"Like hell!" he barked. *"You wouldn't know
a Zen Master if one snuck up behind you
and bit you on the ass!"*
I beg to differ.
I believe I would.
Besides, what kind of Zen Master
goes around
biting people on the ass?
No Zen Master I'd care to know.
That's for damn sure.

Fish Zen
I passed the Zen Master early
one morning as he was dropping
a line into the river.
He bowed to me.
"*Hey, Zen Master, how's it goin'?*" I said,
and kept moving.
I don't have time for all that Zen crap.
On my way home from work,
I passed him again and noticed
that he had caught no fish.
"*No luck, eh, Zen Master?*" I said,
lording it over him.
He shrugged and said, "*It's just as well.
I have no wish to catch fish that have
no wish to be caught.*"
"*Yeah, whatever, Zen Boy!*" I said,
rolling my eyes.
"*Just because you totally suck at fishing,
don't make excuses!*"
He gave me a sad look and I laughed
all the way home.

A Rocky Start
I've only been in one fight
my whole life,
and I handed the guy his hat.
He hit me so hard
his hat fell off.
I was laying there anyway, so
I figured
I might as well hand it to him.
So I did.

Log Cabin
I used to dream a lot about Abe Lincoln.
Most times we'd be at breakfast,
eating pancakes.
Only Abe would never pass the syrup.
I'd ask politely once or twice,
but he'd just give me these odd looks
while munching idly on his
syrup-drenched pancakes.
So then I would say, "*You know, Abe . . .
no one likes a syrup hog.*"
He'd just look at me and start eating again.
Finally, I'd stand up, walk around the table,
pull his stupid hat down over his eyes and give him
a good punch right in the gut.
Then I'd grab the syrup and pour twice
as much on my pancakes as I normally would.
You don't mess with me in my dreams.
I'm a real tough guy.

True Detective
It was a freaky-looking night.
My cat was meowing incessantly.
No matter how many times I said,
"Shut up, cat," he wouldn't.
He didn't seem to care.
I kept waiting
for a shot to ring out,
but it never did.
I fell asleep about midnight.
The next morning, I woke up at ten
and read the paper.
No one got bumped off
during the night.
I decided
to get drunk anyway.

Not What You Think
Sometimes
you're on a ledge so high
all you can do
is fly.

Lightheaded
The newspaper said the President
flew over our town
the other day.
In a helicopter, I assume.
I don't believe he can fly.
If he could, I don't know why
he'd bother being President.
Talk about a waste of time.
Man, I wish I could fly.
If I could, I'd never come down,
except maybe to make a sandwich
or two.
Otherwise, I'd just fly around all day,
weaving in and out of the clouds and
waving to the good folks below.
That would be alright.
Of course, even if I could fly,
I still probably wouldn't get
half as many chicks as The President.
Did I mention he flew over our town
the other day?

My secret plan to rob Fort Knox
1) Find out where Fort Knox is.
2) Go to Fort Knox disguised as a refrigerator repairman*
*Important: Remember toolbox and make sure top fifth of butt crack is showing.
3) Bluff way past main security gate.
4) Go to break room.
5) Unplug refrigerator.
6) Pull out fridge.
7) Pretend to inspect something.
8) Push fridge back into place.
9) Plug fridge back in.
10) Help self to any lunches found in fridge (Hopefully a ham sandwich).
11) Make way to main vault.
12) Tell guards on duty that their voices sound raspy. Watch gleefully as they take twice the prescribed dosage of cough medicine. * Important: Remember cough medicine and also to change the label to TWO teaspoons instead of one. (Make extra sure to keep this a secret, as this is likely a Federal felony).
13) Subtly excuse self. Go back to break room for free government coffee.
14) Return to vault. Tiptoe past sleeping guards. Fill toolbox with several pounds of gold.
15) One last trip to break room for more free government coffee.
16) Resist urge to shout, "So long, suckers!" after driving away from main gate.
17) Nonstop to Vegas!!

A Storm's Harvest
The floor of my heart
is littered with rotting wood,
dead pirate bones
and treasure.

The truth as I see it
Poetry is a sundress wrapped
snugly around a woman.
Everything else
is just
words strung together.

Pirate's Lament
Standing on the shore
surely is a bore.
Better by far to be
out upon the sea.

An American Pirate
Slightly more than two hundred years ago
the mad pirate George Washington—ignoring
the perfectly good advice of Ben Franklin—
crash-landed The Mayflower onto Plymouth Rock.
Then he grabbed an axe, leapt ashore
and chopped down a cherry tree.
When he was finished, his wife Martha—still trying
to straighten her crushed hat—
joined him on the beach.
Washington threw an arm around her,
gestured at the continent laying before them
and shouted, "*Baby, we're home!*"
Then he began chanting, "*U-S-A! U-S-A!*"
Still standing on the bridge of the ship,
Benjamin Franklin shook his head and rubbed
his bald little eyes.
"*Oh, my!*" he said quietly, to himself.
"*England isn't going to like this one bit.*"
He sure got that one right!

Heart of the Matter

Two students took a glass of water and poured exactly half out. Then, being careful not to spill any, they rushed down to the river to find the Zen Master.

They found him meditating by a tree.

"Master!" one cried. "Master, wake up! We have a question for you!"

Slowly, the Zen Master's keen eyes opened. He studied his students placidly.

The student holding the glass smiled mischievously and said, "Master, is this glass of water half-full?"

"Or," said the other, springing the trap, "is it half-empty?"

The Zen Master looked at the glass of water for a moment and replied simply, "I'm not thirsty."

Without another word, he closed his eyes and returned to his meditation.

So you say your grandma's sick
You should just be glad you
have a grandma,
you twisted
son of a bitch.

The Big Conspiracy
No one tells you you're getting fat.
Oh, they'll pass you the gravy,
get you another beer,
and tell you to help yourself to seconds,
but they won't tell you you're getting fat.
Until the day you're in walking in traffic
and someone yells,
"Hey, move your ass, ya fat bastard!"
Then you know.

Says Who?!
There have been times when I've finished
reading a 'classic' book,
stood up, walked to the window,
looked outside at the falling leaves
and felt like someone just kicked
my dog.
And stole my wallet.

Smart
I met this dog the other day.
"*Sit, boy, sit!*" I said.
He didn't.
"*Roll over!*" I said. "*Roll over!*"
He wouldn't.
"*Play, dead,*" I pleaded. "*C'mon, boy,
play dead.*"
He just stood there, wagging his tail,
very much alive.
All he knew how to do was be a dog.
The lucky mutt.

Another trip down memory lane
Back in grade school, I had this friend
who would not
take no for an answer.
I don't know what happened to him.
For all I know, he's still
back in first grade,
wanting to bring
his dog to school.

Demolition Derby
In one of my last dreams,
a man approached me in the rain.
He was holding a hat full of blood.
"*Your hat is full of blood,*" I said.
He shrugged and said, "*It's not my hat.*"
"*But, clearly, it's your blood,*" I said.
"*Bother!*" he said. "*I hadn't thought of that.
Look here, do me a favor, now,
and call me an ambulance.*"
"*Sure thing,*" I said. "*You're an ambulance.*"
"*Excellent, my boy!*" he exclaimed. "*Just so!*"
He beamed and put his hat on.
Blood poured all down his face.
"*These times we live in,*" he muttered,
and wandered off into the night.

The angry young poet revisited
I was at the mall yesterday
when this kid came up to me.
"*I don't believe it,*" he said. "*It's really you!*"
He kept smiling and said,
"*Go ahead, man, say something crazy!*"
"*Aw, I don't do that much anymore,*" I said.
"*C'mon, man,*" he said,
"*rip on those Government bums!*"
I smiled. "*It's not the people,*" I said helpfully,
"*it's the system that's corrupt.*"
He looked at me then with pure hatred in his eyes.
"*You sold out!*" he screamed. "*I hate you! You suck!*"
It's not easy being an angry young poet.
Truth be told, it never was.

Bait and Switch
I screwed up at work last month
and my boss told me I could be
the keynote speaker at
The National Moron Convention.
Then, a week before I was supposed
to leave, he told me there was no
National Moron Convention.
I was kinda bummed out, to be honest.
I had a speech ready
and everything.

About what I thought
I had a gypsy tell my fortune years ago.
She looked at my palm and gave me
a grim look.
"*Your future can be summed up in three words,*"
she said sadly.
"*Loneliness, insanity and gin.*"
I nodded and gave her fifteen bucks.
My friend said, "*That's a terrible fortune.*
Why did you pay her?"
I shrugged and said, "*Gin's okay.*"

Famous Days
My whole thing with fame is
if I knew you before,
I'll know you after.
And if I didn't know you before,
I won't know you after.
So if I didn't know you before,
don't come around after, expecting
to borrow my gui-tar,
because
it's ain't gonna happen!
First of all, I don't have a gui-tar.
Second, why should I borrow it
to you?
Man, I really need an agent . . .

Looking Ahead
People are always asking me if
I'll remember them when I'm
big and famous.
"*Sure,*" I tell them. "*Heck, yeah.
You bet.*"
Deep down inside, though,
I know that when I'm out in California
dating Winona Ryder, and all that sweet
Hollywood dough
is rolling in,
there's no way I'm going to be able to
remember everyone.
Some folks are going to have to go.
I'm not happy about that, but I don't
make the rules.
I just play by 'em.

An Open Letter to J. D. Salinger

Dear J.D.,

I liked your book about The Catcher.
It's one of the best books I've ever read.
But if that's what drove you into
seclusion,
maybe you shouldn't have written it.
I won't argue with you, people
can be awful.
I often wish I wasn't one myself.
Back when I was a kid, I wanted to be
a dolphin when I grew up.
For some reason or other, that never happened.
Anyway, wherever you are, I hope you're okay.
I hope you've found a girl and I hope she
makes you happy.
That's all I got to say.

Your pal,
—Henry

p.s. Could you please sign this and mail it back to me?

Postcard
I'm afraid it hasn't been much of a day.
I've written exactly one poem.
That's one more than Abe Lincoln,
and five less than every other poet
breathing on this planet.
They're out there, in New York, Paris
and Beijing, scribbling away and trying
to make sense of this whole, cosmic hullabaloo.
Not me.
I'm just sitting here having a beer and trying
to figure out a good way to end this postcard.
Well, whaddya know?

Yours,
—Henry

No Escape
The young man sought the Zen Master
far and wide, finally finding him
deep in the heart of a swamp,
sitting on a Cypress stump.
"*Master!*" the young man cried wearily,
"*I am so glad I have found you!*"
"*What is your concern?*" the Zen Master inquired.
"*Tomorrow I am to marry a very beautiful woman,
but I have doubts,*" said the young man.
"*How do I know if she is the right one for me?*"
"*That you have travelled this far
is answer enough,*" replied the Zen Master.
"*Go, my son. Marry.*"
The young man smiled, bowed and then departed.
As soon as he was out of sight, an alligator
surfaced next to the Zen Master.
The Zen Master glanced down at him and said,
"*Do you see what I mean?*"

Revelation
The day I realized I was a poet
I cried for a very long time.
Then I went down to the bar
and drank fifteen full glasses
of beer.
In short order, I found myself raving
to the crowd about the writings of Poe,
Shelley, Byron, Longfellow and other poets
whose works I had never read.
I outlasted every one of them,
chasing the last regular out the door at 1 a.m.,
reciting a poem by W.H. Auden I'd once read
on a subway wall.
Even the bartender was impressed.
He poured me a shot on the house
and I threw it down with a vengeance.
After that, I staggered back to my apartment
and hit the couch.
Before I passed out, I remember thinking,
"You know, I could learn to love this."
Then I passed out.

Pure Crazy
"*Are these poems?*" she asked.
"*I guess so,*" I replied.
She flipped through them again
and said, "*I never realized you
were this weird.*"
I just kind of shrugged.
"*I mean it,*" she said. "*You're pure crazy.*"
I said nothing, only nodded.
Then I stood up and began to move towards her.
"*What are you doing?*" she demanded. "*Get back!*"
I kept on coming.
She said, "*Get away from me, you damned weirdo!*"
I moved closer. She screamed louder.
All at once I reached out,
opened the cupboard above her
and pulled out a box of Fruit Loops.
"*We're out of milk,*" she said distantly,
and went into the living room to watch TV.
Some days were just like that.

"Aristotle, Socrates and Plato are gone. I guess it's just me now."
—Henry Rifle

How to be a Writer—Part 2

by Henry Rifle

So you want to be a writer, eh? Alright. Okay. Fair enough. But you can't first become a writer without first picking up some supplies. Here's what you're going to need:

- One table
- One chair
- One typewriter (Smith-Corona)
- One inkwell
- Black ink (two quarts)
- Six pens (feather)
- One eraser
- Reams of paper (3 or 4)
- Typewriter ribbons (several)
- One Thesaurus
- One Garbage Can (Large)

You'll also want to keep a bottle of cheap gin at the ready—at all times. Once you have these things? You're almost ready to write. Soon, the student will become the master!!

Greatest Hits

Holiday Christmas Wishes—2003
From the desk of
Henry J. Rifle

Greetings, Most Precious of Chums,

Well . . . it's that time of year again when the chronological stew we're all simmering in boils over with goodness and we remove our heads from our butts just long enough to do some power shopping, guzzle some eggnog and whistle a few Holiday tunes.
A-hem! My rampant cynicism aside, it is a very special time of year and I'm truly glad we're all here to share in it together. After all, and I think this goes without saying, it's an uncertain world we're surfing on, truly anything goes, and sometimes the road cheats the wheels, and . . . well, I think you may or may not know what I'm saying. The important thing to keep in mind, of course, is things could be a whole lot worse.

All that aside, this is also the time of year when we as a people simply have to ask ourselves, 'Where are we going?'
Why, just the other day as I was getting on the bus, the bus driver asked me, 'Where are you going?' His question pierced my soul. I had to stop and really think. After about a minute, the other passengers began pelting me with fruit and other debris. The bus driver himself then told me I 'had better sit my ass down' or he was going to 'tear me a new one.' So I took my seat and tried not to look at the other riders who hated me so. But the question hung over them, the same as it hung over me—the same as it hangs over you, my friends. Where are we going?

I'll tell you where we're going: The future. It's our only hope. We have to drop everything right now and make a break for it like there's no tomorrow. There's not a moment to spare—and here's why: I think even the most jaded cynic would admit somewhere in the future things will all make sense. Everything will work just as it's supposed to work, and freedom and justice—and truth—will once again reign supreme. I say, why wait? The sooner we get going, the sooner we'll get there.

If you remember just one thing this Holiday Season, remember this: only by focusing on tomorrow can we hope to forget about today.

All the best to you and yours,

Henry J. Rifle

Bullet Train

"I could never see the future, but I could always see the past. That's why I wore dark glasses."
—Henry Rifle

Bullet Train

by Henry Rifle

All Aboard!
Some people will tell you that
the 60's are over.
That's just The Man,
telling you what he wants you
to hear.
No sir, I'm here to tell you
the 60's are very much alive.
Yep, for some folks
The Free Love Train keeps on
rolling straight through the night.
Any of you Hip Cats
dig what I'm laying down?

Right on.

To My Fellow Passengers
It was sometimes towards fall,
right near the end of summer, 1999,
when it occurred to me that I could
do one of two things.
I could keep hanging around
this boring little party,
sipping watered-down punch and
listening to the god-awful music
or
I could go swing from the chandelier
for a stretch.
My advice to you?
Try the chandelier.
It's excellent.

Greatest Hits

Magic
If you think the world is full
of stupid, pointless people,
you're right.
You'll run into them everywhere . . .
the store, the mall,
the bank, the post office,
everywhere.
But if you stop to think that the world
is full of people
like you,
decent folks getting their asses handed
to them on a daily basis,
but hanging in there, not giving up,
you'll run into them too,
at the very same places
I just mentioned.
It's neat.
Kind of like a party trick.

An old B-side
It seems like every party you go to,
there's always some guy no one wants
to talk to,
and it seems like at every party I go to,
I'm either
stuck talking to that guy or
I am that guy.
Watching movies at home,
now that's where it's at.

Pass the Popcorn
I like movies where the hero gets
betrayed by almost everyone,
has their heart ripped out of their chest,
and then gets kicked, whipped,
stomped, crushed, bruised, battered,
knocked down, banged up, beat up
and left for dead.
Only they don't die.
They hole up, lie low, find their center . . . heal.
Then get stronger and come back
better than ever
to rain hell
on the sons of bitches
who done them wrong.
Romantic comedies are good, too.

Leverage
My whole life I was convinced
The Man was keeping me down.
Yeah, The Man was really
pissing me off.
But then I realized the only man keeping
me down was me.
Only I wasn't really a man; I was just an
overgrown boy.
I only became a man when I finally
let myself up.
Now I'm the man I always wanted to be.
But don't worry.
I won't keep you down.

My Trip to China

My trip to China was fine, I guess.
The people were nice and the rice
was top drawer.
Still, a few things did bother me.
Like that damn wall of theirs.
Everywhere I went, people were all,
"*Hey, Capitalist Dog, have you
checked out our wall?*"
Or, "*Quite a wall, don't you think,
Yankee Bastard?*"
I was polite for a while, but finally
I lost it.
"*Okay!*" I barked. "*It's a Great Wall!
I get it! You folks build first-class walls.
That's terrific. Hooray for you!
I'll keep you in mind if I ever decide
to remodel my basement.
Now can we please all move on
with our lives??*"
It's funny.
No matter where you go,
people always find a way
to annoy the hell out of you.

I mean, Armenian!

I was walking down a Paris street
when three toughs
jumped from the shadows and
began to rough me up.
"*I'm an American!*" I screamed.
Then they
really went to work on me.

The Dark Truth
I wear sunglasses
mainly
to remind folks that I'm cool.
They forget sometimes.

The Fruits of Fame
Except for a couple of
threatening letters, which I likely
would have received anyway,
everyone's been really nice
since Shooting Gallery was released
 a year and a half ago.
Everyone except the Produce Manager
down at the grocery store where I shop.
He's always getting up in my grill.
"*Well, well, look who's here. Mr. Famous!
Isn't this a treat?*" he mutters (though I don't
think he means it).
"*I suppose now that you're famous
you expect a big discount on your produce, huh?*"
"*No*," I reply politely, holding up a ripe orange
for him to see. "*I'm happy to pay full price*."
Which seems to piss him off even more.
He glares at me until finally he sputters,
"*Aw, you Hollywood pricks are all alike!*"

Hooray!
Hollywood exists
nowhere
but in your mind.
The only thing that's real
is the sign.

Slice of Life
The years can either
whittle you down
or make you sharper.
It's all in how
you face the blade.

Discard Pile
For most games,
the jokers don't even
make the deck.
File it under
Sad but True.

Tastefully done, of course
Usually after I write some poems
I like to be in the next county
hiding behind a hedge
when people are reading them.
But after Shooting Gallery was printed,
the first people I showed it to were
my old high school pals.
I just sat in the middle of the room
while they all paged through it around me.
It was like being naked.
I remember thinking it would take
a lot of money
to ever get me to do that.
At least 50 bucks.
Plus expenses.

The best that I could do
This friend of mine is a real piece of work.
He's got this amazing ability to find
almost anything that's lost.
For instance, we were at my aunt's house
once and she was telling me how she'd lost
one of her favorite earring's years ago.
Just as she finished telling me that,
my friend stepped out of the bathroom
and said,
"Has anyone lost an earring recently?"
He's uncanny.
I call him The Finder of Lost Things.
It's all I could think of.

No Static
I was carrying a load of clean laundry
down the hallway of my apartment
when I glanced back and noticed
I had dropped a sock.
So I set the basket down, went back
and picked it up.
I wondered if that's how God operates.
I guessed that it probably was.

Sock and Dagger
This Christmas, I received a pair
of argyle socks.
Digging the look of them,
I wore them to the mall the next day.
After a time, I noticed they were
bunching up, so I put my foot on a display
to hitch them up.
When I did, I heard a voice behind me say,
"Welcome to the struggle, Argyle-brother.
Wait here for further instructions."
Unsure of how to reply, I straightened up
and watched my new friend disappear
into the crowd.
I can't tell you what happened next,
except to say there's more going on
around here than you probably realize.

The Eagle and the Hawk

One fall day, a hawk was perched high atop a tree. Off in the distance, he saw a bald eagle approaching. The eagle soared high, high above the hawk, circling overhead several times before landing gracefully on top of a neighboring tree. The two birds studied one another.

Then the eagle crowed, "Did you see me up there, hawk? Do you see me flying just below the clouds?"

"As a matter of fact, I did," replied the hawk. "You were really something."

"That's right: I am. You could never fly that high, hawk – Never! Do you know why? Because my wings are bigger than yours, stronger than yours, and I can just plain fly higher than you, that's why!"

"True," said the hawk, "but you're bald."

Then the hawk laughed and flew away.

Point Well-Taken
My dad didn't want me
to be a writer.
He always said that writers
go to bed hungry
and wake up thirsty.
Actually, now that I think about it,
maybe it wasn't my dad who said that.
I think it was the guy who lived
down the street.
The fact remains,
a point is a point,
regardless of who makes it.

The name of the game
True artists die penniless
in the street.
Dear God,
how I long
to sell out.

Carry On
There are times when I prefer
vultures to people.
Vultures, at least have the decency
to wait until you're dead before
they start picking at your bones.

Miscommunication

The rookie Coast Guard officer
steered his boat into dock
after his first solo patrol.
Hopping off his boat, he began
to laugh.
The Chief asked him what was funny.
"*I just ran across the coolest customer
anyone will ever meet, Chief.
Here's this guy, right? His boat is
burning AND sinking.
So what does he do about it?
He just sits there, flashing in Morse Code,
'S.O.?' 'S.O.?'
Ain't that about the damndest thing
you ever heard?*"
The Chief just stood and stared.

Overeager

The cell door opened
and the constable and his deputy
entered, peering down at their prisoner,
the pirate who had been terrorizing
their harbor.
"*Well, well,*" said the deputy, mockingly,
"*what have we here? A big, bad pirate, eh?*"
The deputy flashed a cruel grin.
"*Well, just guess where we're taking you
in the morning, Mr. Pirate?
We're taking you to the galley, Matey!*"
The constable smacked the deputy
in the back of the head.
"*Gallows, Stupid,*" he said.

Checkup
The doctor came into the exam room
shaking his head.
"*I won't lie to you, Mr. Rifle,*" he said,
"*you're in terrible shape.*"
I chuckled. "*It's probably my strict regimen
of all beer and no exercise, eh, doc?*"
Then I playfully jabbed his shoulder.
He looked down at his arm distastefully,
as though he'd just been scratched
by an infected lab monkey.
Then he told me not to make any long-term plans
and to enjoy
whatever time I had left.

Legacy
I always keep funny notes
in my pocket in case I
ever get hit by a bus.
That way, whoever gets to me
first
can take them out
and have themselves
a good laugh.

For J. Lennon
Dear IRS,
Please don't tax my monkey.
He doesn't make much dough anyway,
and the forms will confuse him
to no end.
If you would, please grant him
a Section 18, sub-section seven.
The reason we write:
A Monkey Exemption!
Thank you, and we do
hope to hear back
from you
soon.

Feedback Loops
The Beatles pioneered a recording technique
that created sounds which could never be
exactly recreated.
I won't lie and pretend to know how they did it,
but it had something to do
with feedback loops . . .
whatever they are.
Anyway, what they got out of it were
unique sounds,
sounds that had never been made before
and could never be made again.
That's what we are, each of us.
Unique creations that can't possibly be duplicated
as we exist right at this moment.
Wherever you think you are in life
it's important that you hang in there.
Everything one of a kind has value.

Muir Image
My heart is always
feeling best
when it's on the road
and heading west.

And Sometimes it's You
If it were to all end tomorrow,
it wouldn't bother me a bit.
You wouldn't have to feel bad
or anything, because I see how
it all works now,
the way everything fits together.
And for me, it makes as much sense
as it will ever need to.
So even if I get run over by a steamroller
tomorrow, I couldn't complain.
I've had a pretty good run.
Well, except for that steamroller thing.
That's a tough break.
Still, every road
has its bumps.

The Classics Never Die
I love the fact that no matter what,
some things are always going
to be funny.
For instance, it could be the year
2143, and if my head was preserved
in formaldehyde and I saw someone
get hit in the face with a pie,
I'd have to laugh.
"*The old pie in the face bit*," I'd chuckle.
"*What a classic.*"
Of course, I'd have to gurgle that out.
What with my head being
preserved in formaldehyde
and all.

Coney Island
If you think about it,
life is a lot like
a roller coaster ride.
One minute you're screaming,
the next minute you're laughing.
One minute you're crying,
and the next you're just as happy
as a clam.
Then, just as you're getting into the groove,
the ride is over.
And some fat guy is telling you
to 'get moving or it's your ass.'
Yeah, life is simple.
People are always telling you
just what to do.

Life #101
Life begins in a panic
and ends
in a blur.
It's the stuff in between
that can really mess you up.

Life of the Party
I was at this party last night
and this lady came up to me
and said, "*You're drunk!*"
"*Keep it down, lady!*" I hissed.
"*You're going to get me fired!*"

(I'm a banquet server).

A Timeless Lesson

I opened the classroom door and saw the Zen Master in the center of the room, eyes closed, meditating. Trying to be quiet, I inched the door shut while slowly backing out of the room. A split second before it closed, he said, "Enter, my son."

"Damn!" I hissed under my breath. I shoved the door back open and went inside.

"How's it going, Zen Master?" I asked.

"The world is wonderful. How can I be anything but wonderful in it?"

I nodded mechanically.

"And how are you, my son?"

"Oh, you know. The usual. Here when I should have been there and there when I should have been here."

He smiled. "Once you learn that where you are is always exactly where you should be, you will have learned the lesson of a lifetime."

"That's terrific, Zen Master. I'll make a mental note of that."

He looked at me curiously. "You seem troubled, my son."

"Yeah, I'm troubled. I'm troubled big-time!"

"And what troubles you?"

"All this crazy training you have me doing! I mean, come on! Counting our breaths? Chopping down trees with our thoughts? This abstract stuff is getting old. I need something I can lay my hands on—no offense."

He smiled again. "My son, you can only offend me if I agree to be offended, and I choose not to agree. And you're in luck, for today you will be building a wall."

I clapped my hands together. "Alright! Where are the bricks?"

"There will be no bricks. You will build this wall with your mind."

"Alright," I said, "that's it for me. Nice knowing you, Zen Master."

I started for the door but found I couldn't escape his gaze.

"I ask only that you try," he said.

"Okay, fine! You want a wall? I'll build you a wall!" I sat on the floor and crossed my legs. "Now how do I build a wall with no bricks?"

"Let go of what you know," he said. "Let everything go until there is only you, you and a pile of bricks. Then, build a wall."

"Come on," I said, but he cut me off by simply raising one eyebrow.

"Eyes closed," he said softly. "Focus."

While I got started 'building a wall,' I could hear the Zen Master quietly pacing about. "Do not force this," he said. "Build your wall one brick at a time. If you find a brick that doesn't fit, set it down and find another one."

My eyes were closed, but I could picture the wall. It was right there in front of me, just waiting to be built. From there, I lost all track of the clock. Time became meaningless.

Then, suddenly, I heard the Zen Master say, "This is a fine wall, indeed. You have done well."

I opened my eyes and saw nothing in front of me. I was furious!

"If this stuff works for you, Zen Master, I'm glad for you! But it doesn't work for me. I am out of here!!" With that, I strode for the door—but then hit a wall.

And fell backwards.

Little Details
I'm a little bit scared of going out to Hollywood
—for good.
They say you forget about people once
you're out there.
I know for a fact it's true.
Years ago, I went there on vacation
and when I came back,
I no longer remembered my Uncle Louie.
He and my aunt tried for hours
to jog my memory, but nothing helped.
Finally, he sat me down in a chair,
looked me straight in the eye and said,
"*It's me, Henry . . . your Uncle Louie.
You remember your Uncle Louie, don't you?*"
Simply to humor him, I nodded.
"*Sure*," I said. "*Whatever you say, Mac.
Whatever you say.*"

Suffering Succotash
When it comes to romance,
the only person I consider
a contemporary is the Professor
on Gilligan's Island.
We're both decent-looking fellows,
reasonably affable, with generally agreeable
dispositions.
But when that time of night comes around
when both of us should be curling up with
a groovy bird, instead,
the moon finds us in our labs,
conducting bizarre experiments with
coconut shells and stationary bikes.
I'm guessing Nikola Tesla
never got laid much either.

Another Conspiracy
I have a friend we call Lonely Bill.
We call him that because his name
is Bill, and he's lonely.
I don't know what we'll do if he
ever meets a girl.
I guess we'll have to call
another meeting.

Mr. Vegas
I like to gamble.
Yessir, I'm a bit crazy that way.
My friends know it, too.
They call me 'Mr. Vegas.'
Sometimes, though, if you didn't
know better,
it sounds like they're saying
'Mr. Fat-ass.'
But I know better.

Mr. Happy Face
What people want to see more than anything
is a happy face,
and I've got one.
Consequently, everyone digs me.
Okay, not everyone,
but there are a few bad apples
in every bunch.
What are you going to do,
chop the whole goddamn tree down?
George Washington tried that once,
And look where it got him:
Dead in a box.

Do you see what I'm saying?

What it's All About
I've always admired people who
take something negative and
turn it around, make it a positive.
Like the fellow who came home
one night and discovered his dog had fleas.
Instead of flipping out, he wrote a hit tune
about it.
Or that Newton guy who got bonked on the bean
by a falling apple.
Instead of sitting around and moaning about
how unlucky he was, he invented gravity.
Right there—on the spot!
No, I think the best thing a person can do
is use their pain to chart
a new path forward.

Tilt
As soon as I get my time machine perfected,
I'm making a beeline for the 60's.
About the only thing I have left to do
is put shag carpet on the floor
and then it's on to Cal-Berkeley, baby.
Where you can bet that I'll be scoring
like a pinball machine!

Strange But True
Albert Einstein . . .
Mark Twain . . .
Colonel Sanders . . .
I don't know what it is
about funky white hair,
but it sure seems to be
a prerequisite
for genius.

I Guess That's Why . . .
This friend of mine is a blues singer.
Then one day he met a girl
and found he could no longer
sing the blues.
So he lost his job.
And without a job,
he lost his girl.
Now he's
singing the blues again.

Say Cheese!
At the bar one afternoon,
I was watching a television
over this guy's shoulder.
Apparently, he thought I was
looking at him, because he
called out across the room,
"*Why don't you take a picture, pal?
It lasts longer!*"
So I took my camera out
and snapped a quick photo.
It didn't turn out very good, though.
He didn't smile.

Heartfelt
If I ever win an Oscar,
I'll keep my speech pretty simple.
Basically, I'll walk onstage,
grab the award, raise it over my head,
and shout, "*So long, suckers!*"
Then I'll leave early and head over
to Spago, for a big plate of pasta.
While I'm there, I'll do my best to
'pick up' the waitress,
making sure she sees my Oscar.
The statue, of course.
After all, I'm not a Hollywood sicko.
At least not yet.

Hollywood Dreams
I had the coolest dream once.
It was three in the morning and I was
sitting in this sleazy Hollywood diner
waiting for my eggs,
when I glance over and see Dwight Yoakam
sitting a few booths down.
No one else in the whole place but him and me.
I could say something dumb, but for a change,
I decide to play it cool.
Our food is ready at the same time,
and it turns out that Dwight ordered eggs too.
So we both dig in.
I'm like a kid in a candy store.
This is easily the coolest thing—ever.
Finally, I can't take it anymore and say,
"Hey, Dwight, how's them eggs treating you?"
He looks up. *"Real fine,"* he says, with a smile,
and then he goes back to eating, just like that.
I nod in agreement. What a great answer.
And there we are,
two guys eating eggs
in a sleazy Hollywood diner
at three o'clock in the morning.
Which is what it's all about.

Hidden Track
Back when I was a kid, I used to watch
The Six Million Dollar Man with my uncle.
He was unemployed at the time and always
hung out at our house drinking free beer
and watching TV with me.
The Six Million Dollar Man was our favorite show.
It was about a guy who got hurt and the government
subsequently spent six million dollars(!) turning him
into a genuine ass-kicking machine.
Anyway, like I said, while we watched the show
my uncle would help himself to complimentary beers.
Inevitably, at some point in every episode
my uncle would say, *"Six Million Dollar Man, my ass.*
He'd be worth about $3.4 million—after taxes.
Friggin' government."
Then he'd slam the rest of his beer and crush the can.
When he did, he made the same bionic sound
the Six Million Dollar Man made whenever he was
kicking someone's ass.
My uncle was kind of nuts, but he was sure fun
to watch The Six Million Dollar Man with.

Last Stop
One of the first jobs I ever had
I sat across from a guy whose nose
always whistled.
Every time it did,
I'd stand up and shout, "All aboard!"
He never knew what I was talking about,
but what the hell?
It was cheap entertainment.

How to be a Writer—Part 5

by Henry Rifle

Success! You did it! Two months of writing in your spare time and you've finished your first novel! What's more, not one week after typing 'The End,' you've secured a literary agent! And just two weeks after that, your book is on its way to the printing press! This is what it's like to be a writer, my friend (though, to be fair, things usually move a little bit quicker than this). You might think the hard part is over, but you . . . would be wrong! Dead wrong!! Now we get to the hard part: finances. Your debut novel is about to hit the market. Do you A) Play it safe? or B) Assume your book is going to be a best-seller and soon thereafter turned into a major motion picture?

Any writer worth their salt will tell you there's really only one option here: Option B. That economical car you drive? Trade it in for a new sports car. The studio apartment where you hang your hat? It must go. That pricy condo on the Tony side of town is where you need to be. You've sacrificed. You've worked long and hard. You've spent your share of time in the desert. Now? Now it's time to enjoy the fruit of your labors!!

How to be a Writer—Part 6

by Henry Rifle

You're a published writer now and, as a published writer, you must prepare for the inevitable: that moment when you meet John Grisham himself, face to face; peer to peer. Though I've never met the man, meeting John Grisham . . . I'm guessing there's nothing like it in the whole world. But you have to be ready for it. For, in fact, it's not the moment you meet John Grisham. It's the moment that John Grisham meets YOU.

When you see him, wherever you see him (and this will happen), look him square in the eye and turn up the charm to about an 11. Then smile nice and pretty, spread your arms wide and say, "Johnny Grisham, you gorgeous hunk of river meat! Get over here!!"

From there, after an uncomfortably long (for him) embrace, slap him on the back and say, "Hey, I hear you wrote a book called 'The Firm.' What's that all about? Is it some kind of exercise book? If not, what is it about? Just know I don't read paperbacks. But I'll sure check to see if my local library has a copy in Hard Cover. If they don't, I'm sure you have hundreds of unsold copies lying around. Could I just have one of those? Preferably a first-edition?" Before he can answer, squeeze his hand so hard it turns blue, pretend you see someone way more important than him and mutter, "Terrific. I'll have my assistant get you my address." Then give him a light clap on the shoulder and mutter, "See you later, Jack."

And that's it—you did it. You've met John Grisham. Now, was that so hard?

Holiday Christmas Wishes 3 — 2004
From the desk of
Henry J. Rifle

Dearest Chums,

Well, well, well. So another year has passed us by. And as the corpse of the year 2004 begins to decompose and stiffen with rigor mortis, I think all we can do is cut off its clothes, lay it out on the table, examine the skid marks and try to figure out where things went so horribly wrong. Or perhaps it's best simply to dump the whole mess in the cosmic hamper of time and pray that someone somewhere can somehow make it clean.

But . . . enough looking back. I come not to bury Caesar. He died a very long time ago, and if he's not buried by now, man, he has GOT to be some kind of funky! Still, he did invent the wheel and the toga party and was one half of the pioneering comedy team Caesar and Brutus, and for that he should be recalled and recalled fondly.

Which reminds me; the most overused word in the English language today has to be 'pioneer.' I've got a news flash for you: I don't care what you did. Unless you own a covered wagon, you're not a f— pioneer! Let's be real clear about that. And why would you want to be? The pioneers, for the most part, were insane—bloodthirsty pilgrims driven completely mad by the prospect of gold and cheap liquor. But this isn't Thanksgiving we're talking about. It's the Holiday season; eggnog, tinsel, jelly beans and fa la la la.

With that in mind, all I can say is that I truly wish us well, all of us. Life . . . life is a terrifying thing. So for just a few days, at least, can't we try to enjoy it together? Can't we let our guards down and be open even slightly to the prospect of a brighter tomorrow? For all of our sakes, I hope so. Remember, the world isn't driven by courage nearly so much as it's held back by fear. And keep in mind, the heart doesn't come with a kickstand. In these next few weeks and throughout the coming year I encourage all of us to release the parking brake on our souls. I say, let's get these nasty pigs out on the open road and see what they can really do! ARIBA!!

All the best to you and yours,

Sincerely,
Henry J. Rifle

A Bullet West

"Sooner or later, everyone reaches the point where you either have to start taking life seriously or move out to Hollywood."
—Henry Rifle

U.S. $7.95

Henry Rifle

A Bullet West

Henry Rifle

On the Dark Side
My whole life,
I've dreamt of
nothing
but Hollywood.
So you can about
imagine
what my
nightmares are like.

Primer
Hollywood is a glitterbox
full of interesting cats
and nasty
little turds.

Stop

It was late.
Tomorrow had been demoted to today.
A friend and I were at the local truck stop
sopping up beer with French fries and gravy.
Halfway through the meal, I told him I was
thinking about going away.
"*That's great!*" he said supportively. "*Good for you!*
That way you can rest and get the help you need."
"*Moving,*" I said emphatically. "*I'm thinking about moving.*"
"*Oh,*" said my pal, helping himself to my fries.
"*Well, that's good too. You should move. You've been*
a dead letter in this town since I don't know when."
He dipped my fries in my gravy and went on, munching
philosophically as he did.
"*To be honest, you remind me a lot of a dolphin*
in a bathtub. A smart animal—maybe a little too smart—
but one with absolutely nowhere to go."
He grabbed another handful of fries before continuing.
"*Now, in your own environment—if such a place exists—*
you might flourish. Hell, you might even excel.
But around here, you're nothing but a sad curiosity.
Something for kids to poke with sticks."
"*Yeah,*" I said quietly, watching traffic float by on the freeway.
"*Anyhoo,*" he said. "*Where you moving off to?*"
"*Hollywood,*" I muttered.
"*Crackpot Junction!*" he exclaimed, while swiping another fry.
"*Yowza. That's tough competition for crazies, my friend.*
Even for a heavyweight like yourself. Are you scared?"
"*Scared?*" I echoed. "*Sure, I'm scared. Scared of what I might*
do to you if you don't stop eating my goddam French fries."
He grinned and then looked into my eyes.
Then he carefully put the fry back on my plate.
I guess it's true what they say:
Sooner or later, everyone reaches a point where
the line's just got to be drawn.

Robert Leroy Parker

My last day on the job prior to
my big move out west,
the forklift guy
called in sick.
So I got to drive the forklift all day.
It was great!
Man, I was like Butch Cassidy
and The Sundance Kid
rolled up into one big package
on wheels.
With two big forks sticking out
in front of me.

Forks Lift

There was some down time for me
after I quit my job and before
I split for the coast.
In between, I took some time to call some folks
I'd been meaning to call for some time.
Among the people I reached out to was my
Canadian pal up north of the border.
The last I'd heard, he was out of a job
and scrambling to find work.
But when I called him, I learned that
he'd already found a job.
He was happy and relieved to be
working again.
He said it was a metric ton
off his shoulders.

Naive Melody
In one respect, going out to Hollywood
does make me a bit nervous.
I'm just a country bumpkin,
a simple farm boy, see?
I trust everybody.
Until they steal all my stuff
and move down to Mexico.

Then I start to get suspicious.

Play It as It Lays
In a certain sort of way,
I've always thought I'd thrive in Hollywood.
The reason for that? I'm adaptable.
I go
with the flow.
I'm just as comfortable attending a classy
and elegant movie premiere at
Grauman's Chinese Theatre
as I am meeting you for a bare-knuckle
brawl in a back alley
a few blocks
off Sunset.
And if we could do both on the same night,
that would be even more fun!

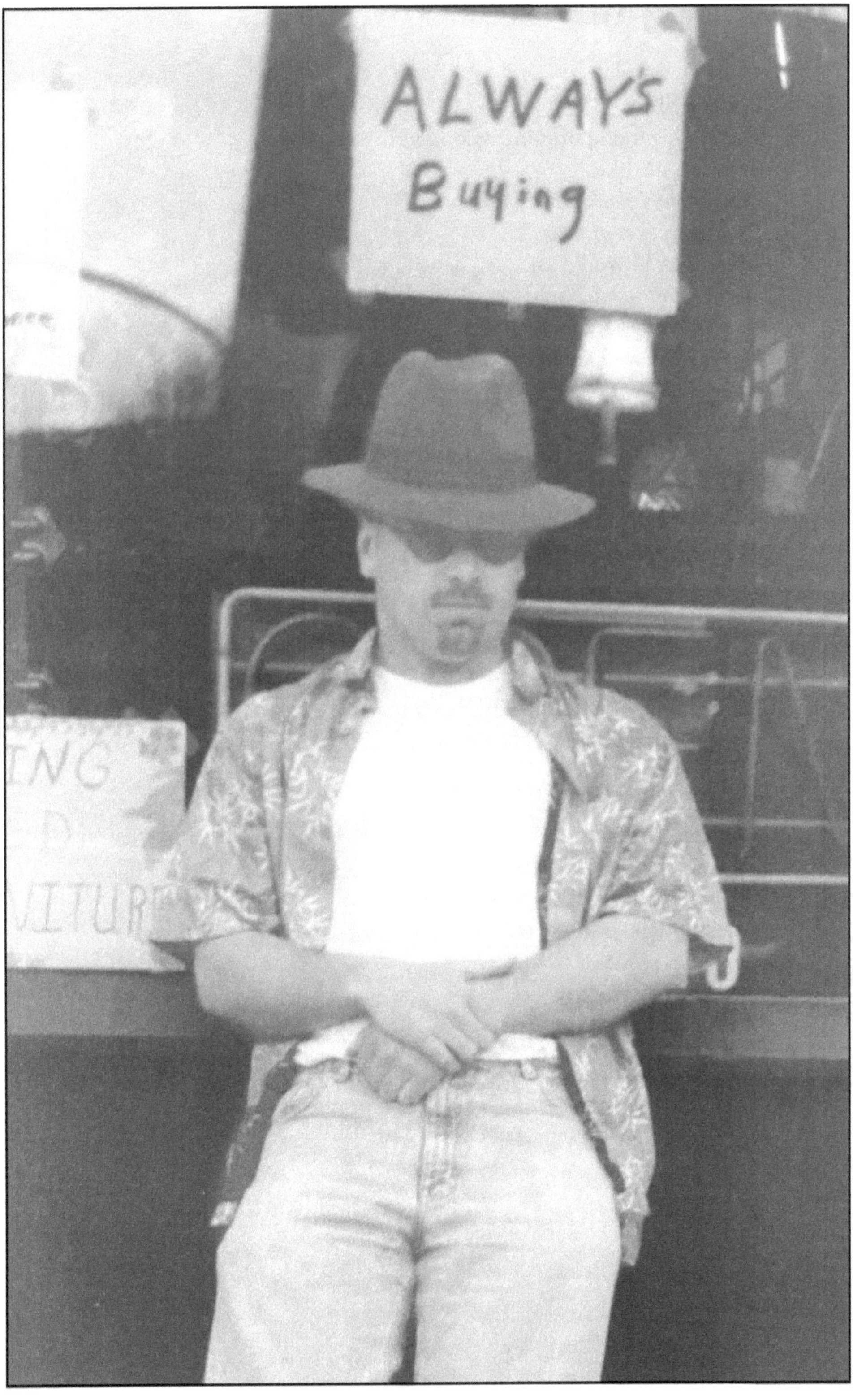
ALWAYS
Buying

Poetry Slam
There's this friend of mine who used to say
things to me like,
*"You know, I don't mind your poetry.
It's alright. Sort of. But . . . "*
"But what?" I would ask.
"But it's just words," he'd say.
*"It's not real. Me, I like things I can feel.
Things I can sink my teeth into."*
"Like what?" I asked.
"Well, like pro wrestling."
So I waited until he turned around and then
I thumped him squarely on the back of his head
with a folding chair.
Now he's one of my biggest fans!

All the Decent People in Hollywood
When I think about all the decent people
in Hollywood,
I can't help but wonder
what they're doing
out in Hollywood.
Hopefully, they just stopped for lunch
and will then continue on with their day
somewhere nice.
Like San Harmonica!
I hear it's pretty down that way.

Breaking News
I strolled into the living room
and found my dad reading
The Wall Street Journal.
"*Hey, Dad,*" I said, "*Guess what?
I'm moving out to Hollywood.*"
"*Absolutely not,*" he said, lowering his paper.
"*It's out of the question and not one thing
you say is going to change my mind.*"
"*But, Dad,*" I said. "*Just think of all the misfits,
weirdos and loonies who've gone to Hollywood
and made millions upon millions of dollars!*"
He looked at me for a moment and then
went back to his paper.
From behind his The Wall Street Journal, he said,
"*Be sure to write. And drive careful.*"

And Worse
I don't like people
knowing where I am
or what I'm doing.
It's not that I'm secretive
or anti-social,
it's just . . . paint your own boat.
I got better things to do.

Something Like This

Whenever I submit my po-ems for publication,
and receive a rejection letter
in return, I always send
a follow-up letter.
They say that's important
in the poetry biz.
My follow-up letters usually go something
like this:

Dear (Name of Magazine),
Your magazine sucks!
I just received your rejection letter,
and I must say, it came as a total surprise.
I don't even remember sending you a poem.
I must have been really drunk that morning.
Because normally I'd know better than to waste
my valuable time on a publication as worthless
as yours.
I wouldn't let my dog read your stupid magazine.
He's a lot smarter than that anyway.
In closing, let me just say again that I think
your magazine sucks and I hope this letter finds you all
rotting in jail, serving three consecutive life sentences.
Period.

Sincerely,
Henry J. Rifle

Probably the Only Thing
One of the few things that
keeps me sane,
as life slams door after door in my face,
is the simple fact that there were once
four guys named The Beatles
who were rejected by every record label
in England before someone finally
saw something in them.
And I don't think I have to tell you
who those four guys went on to become.

Hack
When people found out I was heading out
to Hollywood, they would ask me things
like, "*What are you thinking?*"
and
"*Are you completely insane?*"
One or two asked who out in La La Land
I would most like to meet.
I had to think about that for a bit, until I
realized the person I'd most like to meet
isn't a star or famous.
But rather the person who's been writing my life.
That would be an interesting meeting.
The first thing I would tell them is that they should
seriously consider finding another line of work.
Because they sure as hell
aren't cutting it as a writer.

Traveling Man
Everybody changes the world.
But sometimes the more significant changes
are made by people who've been crushed
at every corner
and smashed at every turn.
Folks who just don't much care anymore
what happens to themselves.
Like Christopher Columbus.
At some point before he and his crew set sail,
I have to think his First Mate or someone
pulled him aside and said, "*Hey, Chris,
don't get me wrong, man.
This New World malarkey is swell and all,
but think about what we're doing!
No one knows what's out there.
We could sail right off the edge of the world!*"
And right then I like to think that Columbus
stared back at him with stainless steel eyes
and said, "*What's your fucking point?*"

Horseshoes for Pegasus
Love can give you wings
and pain
can make you grow them.
Either way, you fly.
How high
and far away
is up to you.

Packing Up
My friend came to visit me just as I was
packing up for L.A.
After I stuffed a dozen cartons of Doral cigarettes
into my travel bag, I piled a couple of pairs of socks,
some underwear and a bunch of shirts on top of them.
"*What about pants?*" she asked.
I shrugged and said I'd figure something out
when I got out to the coast.
"*I can't believe you're going to Hollywood,*" she said.
"*It's a terrible town, Henry. You can't trust anyone,
everyone's for sale and nothing—I mean nothing—
is what it seems!*"
"*Exactly,*" I said. "*It's perfect for me!*"
Then I gave her a Humphrey Bogartesque
knock on the chin.
She was a good egg.
I was going to miss her.

On Being a Bird 2
I'm not the kind of fellow
who likes to wear pressed shirts.
And as for pants,
no thanks.
Birds couldn't fly
if they wore pants,
and, baby, the same
goes ditto
for me!

Greatest Hits

Yoko
She floats on a yes
in an ocean
of no.

8 ½
The Wright Brothers
smashed a lot of
airplanes before
they found one
that could fly.
I did the same thing,
except with lives.

Killer
To whales
who have seen
the blackness of the deep,
the morning light
must seem
miraculous, indeed.

Breakfast in America

There isn't much that's gone
right in my life.
I'm trying to think of one thing.
Anyway, it's no big deal.
After all, there are a few advantages
to going over Niagara Falls
in a barrel and surviving.
Everything after that seems like
Breakfast at Tiffany's.
I'm not kidding.
You could hit me over the head
with a kitchen sink,
stuff me in a burlap sack
and ship me off to Senegal.
The second I regained
consciousness, I'd be thinking,
"*I wonder if I can get
hash browns with this?*"

Brought Again

In this life I was a poet,
and it was okay.
But I wouldn't do it again.
Next time, I'm going to be
a peregrine falcon.
After that,
I'll most likely return as a
10-lb trout.
Then the life after that,
I'll be a pizza guy.
After that, I'm not sure
what I'll do.
I don't like to plan
too far ahead.

Self-Portrait
I'm a strange fish.
What can I tell you?
Blub, blub, blub
—that's me!

Things to Do in Denver
When you're having beers
with ghosts, it's polite
not to speak of the dead.
Ill, well or
otherwise,
they don't want
to hear about it.

Wile E. meets Don Quixote
I'm sure people see
my voyage west and subsequent
search for fame and for-tune
as nothing more
than a quixotic quest
on a chaotic world.
And maybe they're right.
On the other hand,
I've never met a windmill
I thought I couldn't beat.

Journeyman
I've always looked up
to the moon.
Like it or not, you have
to give it its due.
It's hung in there through
thick and thin,
through good times and bad,
and taken shots from damn near
every corner of the universe.
And yet it still drags its ass onstage
nearly every single night
and finds a way to shine.
That's real talent, baby.
And you can't buy it
and you can't rent it.
You either got it or you don't.
Psst: You do.
p.s. Yes, you.

A Touch of Evel
I was blown away
by the Grand Canyon.
It's something you truly do
have to see to believe.
What amazed me most was that
people have attempted to jump
similar traverses with motorcycles.
Looking down, I thought,
"You'd have to be crazy."
But then I remembered that
there are certainly days where
I'd be the first to say,
*"Fire that pig up. I'll show you
a thing or two about
jumping a gravel pit."*
I guess it all depends on
your mood.

Declaration of Co-dependence

The further west I travelled,
the more I realized my trip
was more about about finding out who I was
than it was about getting famous.
You see, shortly before I left home,
I had a serious identity crisis.
I seemed like I was someone
to everyone
but me.
So I called my family and friends
together and told them I could
no longer be all things to all people.
The looks on their faces . . .
it was heartbreaking.
"Alright," I said, *"Who do you want me to be?"*
They all huddled together for a second and
then said, in unison, *"Abraham Lincoln!"*
In response, I reached into my coat pocket and
pulled out a fake beard.
"Fourscore and seven years ago," I began,
as they started to chant,
"Four more years! Four more years!"

When It Began
All of this poetry nonsense
began decades ago
when I was reading a review
of R.E.M.'s album Monster.
I was a big R.E.M. fan then—and
still am—and in the review, the
reviewer said that on that album,
R.E.M., quote, 'rocked harder'
and 'rocked weirder.'
Enraged, I hurled the magazine
away.
I wanted to rock harder.
I wanted to rock weirder.
Unfortunately, I didn't know anything
about music. Still, something had to be
done—but what?
Then it hit me: I liked to drink and was
pretty good with words . . . why not
become a poet?
From there, I picked a mock-tough name
and the rest is pure history.

Aisle 51
There's never really
a bad time to work
at a grocery store.
But I'm sure there are times
that are more fun than others.
Like Halloween!
I'd love to be a Store Manager
that time of year.
I'd offer all kinds of fun/spooky
promotions.
Like, Haunt Jemima syrup, $3.19.
R.I.P.ples potato chips, $3.99.
And of course, 'Dead' of Lettuce . . .
$.99.

Tools of the Trade
This is just my opinion,
so take it for what it's worth,
but I think everyone
ought to have a
bullshit Hollywood story.
Really.
My bullshit Hollywood story
is that I produced Blondie's
classic single, Heart of Glass.
It's no big deal.
The band deserves
a lot of credit too.

Role Playing
When I was younger, I used to
hang out with my older brother
and one of his best pals.
That cat was nuts!
He was always coming up with
the craziest ideas.
We'd be sitting around and he'd say,
"I know! Let's play 'Rock Star!'
I'll be the rock star, you (my bro)
can be my brilliant manager,
and Danny (what they called me then)
can be the sniveling weasel from
the record company!"
"Aw, no fair!" I would complain.
"I always have to be the sniveling
weasel from the record company!"

Down in Front
When I was out in Hollywood,
I was front man in a band.
We were solid, man. Tight.
Then one day I was talking
to this Canadian singer
and he said something interesting.
So I went back and told my bandmates
all about it.
I said, "*Guess what, fellas? Old Mike Plume
finally hooked up with a band!
Yep. Apparently, he's caught on with an
existing group, one whose lead singer
just isn't cutting it. A real hack—if you will.
Oh, and just guess what that prima donna
Plume is going to name his band!*"
Everyone just stood there, silent.
I remember thinking it was strange.
No one in The Henry Rifle Band
even wanted to take a guess.

Way Behind the Music
I'm glad The Henry Rif-
I mean, The Mike Plume Band
had such a wonderful run.
Why shouldn't they have?
They're all great guys and terrific
musicians.
I'm happy for them.
I always have been.
Because it wasn't about me.
It never was.
It was about the music.
It was about . . .
It was about . . .

(EDITOR'S NOTE: At this point in the interview, Mr. Rifle began to sob uncontrollably. He was helped to the parking lot, where he was found the next morning—still crying. He was then helped into a taxi cab).

Death Cab for Cutie
It had been a terrible day.
I was in the backseat of a cab
and we were stopped
at a red light.
I glanced down and saw
an aluminum can
smashed flat
in the gutter.
I thought, "*I know exactly
how that can feels.*"
And then the light
turned green.

Attitude
It was the same cab, same ride.
At a different red light,
my cabbie glanced down at his newspaper
for just a second, and the light turned green.
Immediately, the driver behind us blared
their horn.
That's always the way of it, I swear.
You can stare at a red light forever,
and it won't change.
But as soon as you look away, for any
reason at all, it turns green as if to say,
"*Here's your green light, Tito.*
Now everybody hates you.
How do you feel about that?
about that?
about that?"
And I don't know about you,
but nothing pisses me off more
than a traffic light calling me
'Tito.'

Rotary Club
Throwing stones at the moon
doesn't make you a meteor shower.
On the contrary, it most likely
just means
you have too much time
on your hands and
too many stones
at your disposal.

Dotted Line
Growing up, I had this cousin
and more than anything in the world,
he wanted to sign a recording contract
with RCA.
It's all he ever talked about,
morning, noon and night.
He never did get that contract with RCA,
but now he's a contract killer
for the CIA.
So don't tell me that things don't
work out for the best.
Mister, I don't want to hear it!

Western Dressing
My cousin and I were having salads
on a restaurant patio.
All at once, he looked up and frowned.
"*Hm,*" he said. "*I don't like the looks of
that satellite.*"
He went inside to make a call while I
looked up at an empty blue sky.
When my cousin returned, he said,
"*Don't worry. I made a call.
It's one of ours.
Go ahead, enjoy your salad.*"
I tried, but as I munched on a crouton,
I couldn't help but feel like
a gas station weenie rotating ceaselessly
in pointless circles.

You Tell Me What It Means
I think everyone should have
a far-out friend
at least once before
the government kills them.

Life Imitating Art
Before I moved to Hollywood,
I couldn't stand foreign films.
Mainly because they reminded me
too much of my own life
at the time.
Nobody spoke my language,
I couldn't figure out why anyone
was doing any of the things they were doing
and it seemed like everyone
was scoring
except for me.

Radio Silence
It was a Friday night in Hollywood.
My buddy called me up and said
we should pick up some ladies
and go out dancing.
I said I couldn't.
He asked why not.
I told him it was because I had
sprained my ankle earlier in the day
trying to get El Debarge's autograph.
There was no response.
"*Hello?*" I said.
"*Hello?*"

Vapor Room
If you fart
in an empty room . . .
at least you're not alone
anymore.

Comforter
If you're worried about
being cool,
you can relax.
You're not.

Subtraction
You disappear a bit
each day
until the day
you're gone.

Addition
Love is very Boolean
in nature.
Two plus two is rarely
four.
In fact, it's often
seven.

Fractions
I used to avoid pain.
Walk miles out of my way
to duck out on getting hurt.
That's all changed.
I'll take all the pain you have now,
everything you got,
and I'll find a place for it
somewhere.
It doesn't matter anymore,
because, between you and me,
I've almost completely dissociated
from myself.

It's true.
He has.

Industrial Cookie
Life isn't easy.
It can be rough.
Until you figure out
the right balance
of tender and tough.
It's an inexact science
at best.

Rule of Three
Growing up,
my heroes were
J.D. Salinger, Bobby Fischer
and the Loch Ness Monster.
Cats who understood the game
and knew just how to play it.

Keeping My Cool in Madison

I like Madison, WI.
It's a real neat town.
I was there one winter
on an icy, cold day
only to discover I'd lost
one of my gloves.
So what I did, was put the glove I had
on one hand and then put
my bare hand in my coat pocket,
thus completing the illusion.
When I got down to State Street,
All the young hippies were flipping.
"*Check out the cat with two gloves!*"
they exclaimed.
"*He's the coolest!*"
And I continued along on my merry way,
thinking quietly,
"*Suckers . . .*"

Good Humor

If a movie star and an ice cream truck
were going opposite ways
down the same street,
the only ones who would always know
which one to chase are kids
and dogs.

Craft
If I were a lumberjack,
I might say things like,
'the teeth of time are sharp,'
and 'it's the quiet buzzsaws
you have to watch out for.'
But I'm not a lumberjack.
Still, there are days where I'd like
nothing more than to take an axe
to my past.
And days like those are tough,
but you learn to live with them.
They make you who you are.
Do I wish I could have avoided
some of the thrashings I've taken?
Sure.
I mean, love taps are nice.
They provide definition.
But make no mistake,
it's the hammer blows
that shape you.

Insufferable
Sure, I could probably be
doing more to make myself
a success.
But you know what?
To succeed in your eyes
would be to fail in my own.
And these are the eyes
I have to look through
each and every day.
Plus,
I really like
to watch TV.

Fame
Fame is like rain
on a sunny day.
Interesting,
but you know
it can't last.

Fame 2
And why would you want it to?
The sun is the star
of this production, pal.
All you're doing is sucking up
free heat and light.
So why don't you go back
to The Beverly Hills Hilton,
put on your stupid sunglasses
and sit by the pool?
We'll tell you when it's time
for your close-up.

Black Riding Hood
One of the great tribes of
the Pacific Northwest
has a legend that says
the killer whale is a wolf
who got lost out at sea.
I love that story because
it's simple.
And because it shows very clearly
that even though the world is
oftentimes a prison,
flexibility is key.

Gloomy Tunes
Whenever that damn coyote
falls off the cliff,
he's no longer the same
creature.
Something is added each
and every time.
Even if it's only another layer
of dust
and matted blood.

Disclaimer
I really don't smoke
anywhere except
in my dreams.
It helps me think better.

Small Blessing
The things that make us famous
rarely keep us famous.
And for that, we should
be thankful.

Blossom
If you ever take a class
from The Buddha
and he holds up
a flower,
smile.
It's the right answer.
All you have to do, then,
is figure out why
it's the right answer.
It's not that hard,
and when you put it
together, the smile
is yours to keep.

Spare Time
I like to take things apart,
put them back together
as best I can
and then try and return them
for a cash refund
claiming the salesperson
didn't give me a receipt.

That's what I like to do.

Upside Down in the Spoon
There are times I think
that being famous
is like discovering
the Lost City of Atlantis
in your bathtub.
Sure, the attention is nice,
but most nights all you
really want to do
is take a nice, hot bath
and go to bed.

Dave Addison
There's nothing better than
a crazy hero.
One who cares—but
doesn't care
—in equal parts.

"I hope to leave the world a bitter place. That's not a typo."
—Henry Rifle

Crystal Clear
I had my fortune read again
out in Los Angeles.
It had been a few years.
The fortune teller looked deep
into her crystal ball
and said, sadly, "*I see only loneliness—*"
"*insanity and gin,*" I said,
completing the grim prognosis for her.
She said, "*You have The Gift!*"
"*It's no gift,*" I muttered.
"*All it is, is connecting the dots
to make a picture.*"
After giving her a twenty,
I stepped outside and found myself
in front of the famed Whisky a Go Go.
I put on my sunglasses and
went inside.
It all sounded pretty good
to me.

Look Homeward
They named a street after me
back home.
It's a dead-end street.
Unpaved.
More of a drainage ditch, really.
An old sewage canal.
I haven't decided if I'm going to
attend the dedication ceremony
or not.
I think it might
be a trap.

Oh, Don't Be Wan
It was springtime.
I was a budding poet, so they
brought me in to the classroom
to 'rap with the kids.'
Me allegedly being hip and all.
Being as clueless as anyone else
when it comes to speaking to kids,
I asked 'em what they wanted to be
when they grew up.
All around the room they gave me
fine answers, like doctors and lawyers
and such.
Until we got to a kid in the back
of the room, who said he wanted to be
a bowl of cornflakes
when he grew up.
The other kids laughed and the teacher
pooh-poohed him,
but I thought to myself,
"The Force is strong in this one."

Yogi
Statistically speaking,
your chances of becoming
a famous bear
are much better than
your chances of becoming
a famous human being.

Henry 5.0
The shadows have been my friends
low these many years,
they've kept me hidden well.
But now the time has come
to say goodbye
and trade my gray
for blue skies.
My black
for yellow sun.

"I'm not afraid to drink yesterday's coffee or smoke tomorrow's cigarettes. I seek balance in everything that I do."
—Henry Rifle

Housecleaning
It would have been easy
to stay in L.A.
Part of me will always wonder
if I made the right choice.
But I'd been away long enough.
What settled it for me was something
the Zen Master said as I
showed him around my jazzy
West Coast apartment.
I thought he would like it,
but when I asked him what he
thought, he simply said,
*"An empty room with a view
might as well be a broom closet."*
Then he bowed and shuffled off
for tea.
Smiling ruefully, I sighed and began
to take my pictures off the walls.

Greatest Hits

Holiday Christmas Wishes 4 — 2005
From the desk of
Henry J. Rifle

My Dearest Muchachos,

It appears we are rapidly running out of days on the calendar to draw thick, black X's through, so that can only mean it must be time for old Henry J. to put fingertips to keys and tap his way back into the fibrous chambers of your hearts. Don't worry, it will only sting for a minute and I promise you won't feel a thing.

Now before I get too far down that happy path, I should tell you I just got back from a Holiday party and I'm pretty sure someone spiked the egg nog. Did I stop drinking it, you ask? The answer, of course, is no, I did not. So why don't we just let's see what happens? Well, it was quite a year. As some of you know, I was bumped off earlier this year, rubbed out like a 2nd-rate soap opera star*. It's alright, though. It's given me time to catch up on my reading. And I've seen a movie or two. Yep, I saw Walk the Line recently. Not too bad, not too bad at all. If you like Johnny Cash, you'll be happy to know the movie has a happy ending. In fact, it ends (spoiler alert) with Johnny's landmark performance in Folsom Prison, a performance which was later turned into the equally landmark-tic album, 'Folsom Prison Blues'. Yes, after listening to that album, it's obvious nothing coaxes a better performance out of a performer than the knowledge he'll be torn to pieces by hardened cons if he sucks.

Luckily for all of us, and most especially Mr. Cash, he did NOT suck. And the album? It went gold! Or platinum . . . I never remember what the difference is. Anyway, this business of artists performing in prisons caught on very briefly. It led, regrettably— and nearly fatally—to the legendary lost recording titled, 'Perry Como, Live from Alcatraz!' I'm sure that seemed like a real good idea at the time, and big points to Perry for trying. But apparently, he didn't quite have the all-important 'street cred' old Johnny Cash did. Still, that's how you learn, right?

Henry Rifle

Oh, sure, everyone and their great-aunt thinks they can pull on a turtleneck sweater, pick up a guitar and entertain a bunch of hardened criminals. The bottom line is, however, we can't. There's only one performer (two if you count Merle Haggard) who was mean and crazy enough and had the chops to do that. And now . . . he's no longer with us. Anyways, Happy Holidays!

All the best to you and yours,

Sincerely,
Henry J. Rifle

* *In the beyond-indie film Henry Rifle is Dead*

Who Are You? (Doot-Doot-Doot-Doot)

My last night in Hollywood, I ran into
another sad case down on Sunset Boulevard.
It was nighttime, the stars were snug
in bed.
I hitched up my worn jacket collar
and shuffled wearily up to the crime scene,
sipping on stale cup of joe.
"*What do we got, Lieu?*" I asked.
Staring grimly down at the body,
the lieutenant said,
"*Male victim, early 30's. Cause of death:
Blunt force trauma to the head.*"
I shook my head and stared out to sea.
I couldn't see it from where I was standing,
but I knew it was out there, somewhere.
"*75 degrees in the shade,*" I muttered,
each word layered in jade,
"*and this town just keeps getting colder.*"
Glumly, he nodded in agreement,
then stared at me for a long moment.
"*Hey, who the hell are you?*" he demanded.
With that, I tossed my paper cup aside
and sprinted off into the night.

"I'm not sure what the future holds, but I'm willing to bet—whatever it is—it will club me over the head with it."
—Henry Rifle

The Nudie Blues
Would I ever come back?
Perform again as Henry Rifle?
That's tough to say.
Though I can tell you,
the only way I would even
think about doing it is if
I could rock a rhinestone-encrusted,
baby blue
Nudie suit.
If not, then forget about it.
You can keep Henry Rifle.
He's all yours.
Maybe you'll have better luck
with him
than I did.

Popular Misconception
People always thought I was
this gritty, greedy miser.
But I wasn't greedy!
I was never greedy.
All I wanted was ten percent.

Of everything.

The Old Ballgame
(The Ballad of Shoeless Joe Jackson)

Shoeless Joe Jackson liked wearing shoes
as much as anyone—perhaps even more so.
And he LOVED playing baseball in shoes.
It was his jam.
Until one day a group of greedy baseball owners
got together and decided it would be funny
if they forced him to play without shoes.
And, also, to go without shoes
in his day-to-day life.
That's how that whole shoeless business began.
And it just kept going like that, for years.
Up until the day Shoeless Joe finally threw down
the gauntlet and told the greedy owners
he was going to start wearing shoes again.
The greedy owners warned him that if he did that
they would wait until his team got into the
World Series and they would put the fix in
and pin all the blame squarely on him,
adding that no matter how well he played,
he would take the fall for their misdeeds.
Also, the greedy owners mentioned, 'We'll make more
money on the deal than you can imagine, Shoeless Joe.
More money than you can even dream of!'
Shoeless Joe said, "That's insane. You'd never
go through all of that just to keep me from
wearing shoes. It's outlandish. It's . . . preposterous!!"
The greedy baseball owners just smiled.
Within two months, Shoeless Joe's team
had lost the World Series.
He himself was disgraced
and soon forced out of baseball altogether.
As for the greedy owners, they were far richer
than they had been in all of their privileged lives.
Shoeless Joe Jackson, on the other hand,
never wore shoes again.
He couldn't afford them.

Henry Rifle

He died penniless—and barefoot—in an alley
behind a cobbler's shop.
But, that's the way the ball bounces.

Final Assessment
I don't really fit in
and I never will—fit in.
Not until the end and that last,
six-foot trench gets cleanly filled.
And that's fine with me.
I just wish I had known that
and been okay with that
years and years ago.
It would have spared us all
a lot of headaches.
And a whole bunch of
moonlit poems.

Commencement Address
It's a big,
stupid world.
Good luck out there.

"I'll probably never write War and Peace. But to be fair, I'll probably never read it, either."
– Henry Rifle

How to be a Writer—Part 7

by Henry Rifle

You've already learned so, so much. Under my tutelage, you've gone from someone who couldn't even type to someone who has met John Grisham in person AND written a best-selling novel. You better pinch yourself—just to make sure you're not dreaming!! Now, unless that pinch snapped you out of this literary wonderland, there's only two or three steps left to go. I'm going to keep it pretty simple: Why did you start writing? The answer, of course, is money. Few vocations are as profitable as writing creatively and you wanted your share of the largesse. It makes perfect sense.

And now? Now you're in the catbird seat. It's time to talk about the sweetest plum of all—the advance. The pile of money a publisher is going to hand you (interest-free) for the rights to your next masterwork. You get one shot at this, Tolstoy. One shot, Sylvia Plath. DO NOT BLOW IT!! What you'll want to do is play it close to the vest. Tell your literary rep you have a dynamite concept. Tell them the follow-up book is practically writing itself, but add that you can't say more; you don't want to jinx it. This is when you have to bury your pride at sea and really sell it. Lay it all on the line! Meanwhile, are you actually doing any writing? Hell no! What are you, some kind of machine? There's only one Stephen King and he resides in Bangor, Maine. The best that you can do (and me, too) is to pretend you have another idea as good as the one that drove your first book. It's time for the piper to be paid and for once in your whole, damn unprofitable life, you're the piper!

However, as this is all playing out, you do need to do some work. Start building a new identity on the side. Pick up some wigs, theatre makeup and clothes unlike anything you've ever worn or would wear. Think about a name you could grow into—a whole new persona. You're probably wondering, Is all this in preparation for pocketing your advance and vanishing into thin air? Here's my unvarnished answer to that: You're g-damn right it is.
You really are learning, you know that?

The cover photo of Henry Rifle's legendary lost volume of poetry, "Henry Rifle Slept Naked Here".*

*This book is exceptionally rare. Finding a copy in any condition is akin to finding a pristine Gutenberg Bible with a mint condition Honus Wagner baseball card tucked inside—signed by J.D. Salinger.

Green Light Blues

If you can, I want you to picture a single traffic light. From there, I want you to imagine dinosaurs, great and small, roaming past that traffic light—which is a steady green, by the way. Then I want you to picture a flash of light, an immense explosion and a sky turned to fire. The dinosaurs all disappear and a dense, smoky cloud hovers over the whole planet. Still, far beneath those darkened skies, that light remains a steady green.

Then I want you to picture sheets of ice slowly encroaching, eventually covering everything in a deep, thick, crystalline blanket. Even so, if you looked hard enough down through that ice at a certain angle, you'd pick up a hint, the tiniest speck, of green.

After several centuries, the ice melts and huge inland seas are formed. Mountains rise off in the distance, and immense valleys are eventually carved between them as inland oceans become too large to hold, breaching massive earthen dams on their way out to sea. After the water is gone, the traffic light is exposed once more. Buffalo and Native Americans eventually begin to roam past on the prairie, then explorers and finally settlers steadily moving west. All of them glance up at the glowing green light and wonder what it could mean.

Finally, after railroad lines and countless trains have passed through and, later still, roadways have been plotted, laid out and constructed—with that traffic light a constant green throughout every change—I come tooling along in my beat-up jalopy. And, just as I reach that traffic light . . . it turns red.

PROJECT SUMMARY

In terms of commercial success, The Henry Rifle Project was a complete and utter failure. From a profit and loss standpoint, the historical scales will forever tilt heavily toward loss. Still, more than anything else, Henry Rifle was a lifeboat launched by a man who was sinking rapidly. An emergency buoy fired up from the depths.

Even if that lifeboat never reached new worlds and did little more than drift about in vast and empty seas, the fact of it is, it kept its lone occupant afloat—alive.

From that viewpoint and that viewpoint alone, The Henry Rifle Project was an unqualified success.

Books by Henry Rifle*
Shooting Gallery (1998)
Bullet Train (2000)
A Bullet West (2002)
Ballistics Report (2011)

Books by Dan Hendrickson**
Clean Shorts (1994)
The Portland Stories (*Clean Shorts*—reprinted with a more apt title) (2000))
Dark Glasses (2017)
Comedy Album (2020)

Beyond-Indie Films***
Henry Rifle is Dead (2005)
Nonsense is My Chicken (2022)

* Henry Rifle is Dan Hendrickson
** Dan Hendrickson was once Henry Rifle
***Find them on YouTube.

Henry Rifle was a pseudonym once used by Dan Hendrickson, although that particular fictional construct has now largely been abandoned—like an out of service railroad line. While in operation, Henry Rifle produced four books of poetry: *Shooting Gallery, Bullet Train, A Bullet West* and *Ballistics Report*. In this tongue-in-cheek "Greatest Hits" collection (if you will), *Ballistics Report* is represented only by the poem "Who Are You?" Which is not to say it's a bad book. On the contrary, it's the most evolved of the whole bunch. Some people have gone so far as to say they kind of liked it.

As for Dan Hendrickson, he lives in Minneapolis with his family and continues to write below the radar, off the wall poetry under his own moniker—and also dabbles with screenplays. Though it doesn't happen often, he enjoys getting paid.

Henry Rifle <u>will</u> return (maybe)

www.ingramcontent.com/pod-product-compliance
Lightning Source LLC
Chambersburg PA
CBHW020426010526
44118CB00010B/438